Berkshire Poets

Edited By Donna Samworth

First published in Great Britain in 2018 by:

 Young**Writers**

Young Writers
Remus House
Coltsfoot Drive
Peterborough
PE2 9BF
Telephone: 01733 890066
Website: www.youngwriters.co.uk

FOREWORD

Welcome, Reader, to *Rhymecraft - Berkshire Poets*.

Among these pages you will find a whole host of poetic gems, built from the ground up by some wonderful young minds. Included are a variety of poetic styles, from amazing acrostics to creative cinquains, from dazzling diamantes to fascinating free verse.

Here at Young Writers our objective has always been to help children discover the joys of poetry and creative writing. Few things are more encouraging for the aspiring writer than seeing their own work in print. We are proud that our anthologies are able to give young authors this unique sense of confidence and pride in their abilities as well as letting their poetry reach new audiences.

The editing process was a tough but rewarding one that allowed us to gain an insight into the blooming creativity of today's primary school pupils. I hope you find as much enjoyment and inspiration in the following poetry as I have, so much so that you pick up a pen and get writing!

Donna Samworth

CONTENTS

Katie Fidler (9)	71	Valentina Aurora Prestel (7)	113

Katie Fidler (9) 71
Georgia Fairchild (10) 72
Rubi Loughnane (10) 73
Jayden Fry (9) 74
Matthew Cox (10) 75
Kiera Peacock (10) 76
Kiran Acharya (10) 77
Reema Muhajireen (10) 78
Shivani Gurung (10) 79
Jorja Evans (10) 80
Danny Mark Eaton (9) 81
Navarro Graham (9) 82
Jasmita Sehra (10) 83
Urwa Nazir (10) 84
Ryan Smith (11) 85
Kai Furnivall (10) 86
Mason James Hale-Cox (9) 87
Dylan Hancock (10) 88
Rayann Malluna (10) 89
Ayrton David Stewart (11) 90
Keyessence Montaque (10) 91
Alannah Louise White (10) 92
Kevin Tuleassi (10) 93
Ela Erceri (10) 94
Ledlie George-Kwaku Otu (9) 95
Ellie-Rose Barnes (10) 96

Oldfield Primary School, Maidenhead

Ella Weaving (7) 97
Oliver Green (10) 98
Isabelle Gorf (10) 100
Nina Jasmine Harris (10) 102
Jaya Doshi (9) 103
Leah Johnston (10) 104
Eva Johal (7) 105
Esha Dosanjh (9) 106
Niamh Campbell (9) 107
Ellie Schlotterbeck (8) 108
Riyan Hoque (7) 109
Emily AJ Wood (7) 110
Jasmin Bouri (7) 111
Scarlett Storm (7) 112

Valentina Aurora Prestel (7) 113

Our Lady's Preparatory School, Crowthorne

Addison Faux (7) 114
Maria Clayton 115
Jacob Clay (7) 116
Victoria Miller (10) 117
Eloise White (7) 118
Caitlin Ure (10) 119
Jayden Berdat (7) 120
Harry Westland (9) 121
Leo Kimani 122
Ruby Morgan (7) 123
Alyssa Alexandra McDougall (7) 124
James Ferguson 125
Elijah Kayanja (8) 126
Sam Spiro (7) 127
Chloe Norgate (7) 128
Izzy Rae (7) 129
Connie Wall (9) 130
Liberty-Grace Harrod (8) 131

Park Lane Primary School, Tilehurst

Sreevedha Bhuvaneshwaran 132
Libby Heather Jones (9) 134
Jack Purvis (9) 135
Maya Dahunsi-Poulsen (9) 136
Ruby Allen (7) 138
Ria Ahuja (8) 139
Avi Srivastava (10) 140
Anthony Ribbons (9) 141
Amelia Sue Rain (9) 142
Kyra Louise Yanni (8) 143
Ella Wilson (8) 144
Demi Paris Brockbank (7) 145
Kurinji Srinivasan (8) 146
Grace Annetts (9) 147
Moksha Pallapothu (8) 148
Grace Taylor (10) 149
Tess Lawrence (8) 150

Lily May Dimes (8) 151
Renae Sebogiso (10) 152
George O'Connell (7) 153

St Margaret Clitherow Catholic Primary School, Pembroke

Erin O'Donovan (10) 154
Niamh Clyne (8) 155
Jarrell Cardoz (11) 156
Alea Doua Mchala 157
Valerie C Ustariz Rodriguez (10) 158

Streatley CE Primary School, Streatley

Eloise Hanson (10) 159
Fergus Joseph Caulfield (10) 160
Cai Iestyn Davies (10) 162
Joanne Roy (10) 164
Sacha Webb (11) 165
Fraser Cox (10) 166
Euan McInnes (11) 167
Ella Von Sternberg (9) 168
Jay Radbourne (11) 169
Cory Forder (9) 170
Ben Howe (10) 171
Emily Richardson (10) 172
Elsie Waite (10) 173
Jacob Steer (10) 174
Gus Dellowe (11) 175
Emily-Jayne Victoria Moore (9) 176
Annabel McLean (109) 177

The King's House School, Windsor

Caleb Josiah Navarro (8) 178
Leo Bello (8) 179
Abigail Simpson (10) 180
Joshua Richards 181
Lydija Christine Rademeyer (8) 182
Harry Wood (8) 183
Micah Odufuwa 184
Hope Simpson 185

Isaac Johannes Wesley Erasmus (8) 186
Benjamin Harding (10) 187
Jeshurun Ali 188
Reuben Andrew Harding (8) 189
Joseph Richards (10) 190
Levi Swart (7) 191
Kian Van Der Merwe 192

Willow Primary School, Fernside

Arpan Kaur Atwal (10) 193
Imaan Jalil 194
Hammad Khalid (11) 196
Aleeza Habib (8) 197
Milena Bielawska (11) 198
Bikramjit Singh Somal (9) 199
Bisma Zafar (8) 200
Nadia Ankiewicz-Heetun (8) 201
Navsirat Singh (10) 202
Skeena Zara Shah 203

THE POEMS

Everyone Knows

Nobody has to know I'm quick.
Nobody has to know I'm smart.
Nobody has to know I'm strong.
Nobody has to know I'm in love with gold.
Nobody has to know my favourite car is a Ferrari.
Nobody has to know I love babies.
Nobody has to know I'm good at football.
Nobody has to know I'm the third one to get milk
every day.
Nobody has to know I'm the last in school.
Nobody has to know I'm a bookworm.
Nobody has to know I'm good at poems.
Nobody has to know I'm lazy.
Nobody has to know I'm a sporty person.

Tyrell Jordan (9)
Geoffrey Field Junior School, Reading

Seasons

Winter, soft snow everywhere,
All the trees are looking bare.
Winter, cold and snowy,
Also very blowy.

Spring, all the animals are being born,
It is sworn,
To be the best,
The time that a bird makes a nest.

Summer, very hot and fun,
The season of the sun.
Time to eat an ice cream
While the sun gleams.

Autumn, getting colder each day,
The perfect time to play,
So all the seasons come and go
From sun to snow.

Helena Knuts (8)
Geoffrey Field Junior School, Reading

Four Seasons Of The Year

Winter is starting and I'll be iced.
Day will be short, like a blink of an eye.

Spring is coming and birds are singing.
Flowers start to bloom with the splash of a rainbow.

Summer is on its way with a long, long day.
Hot, hot, hot with fun and BBQ days.

Autumn is here, taken everything away.
Wind is being crazy, blowing leaves like rain.

Zoraez Imran (8)
Geoffrey Field Junior School, Reading

Oh My Fluffy Cat

Oh my fluffy cat,
It's time to catch a rat.
Oh my fluffy cat,
Don't just sit on a mat.

The rat is very cheeky,
It might be very squeaky.
It goes as fast
As a pirate on a raft.

Oh my fluffy cat
Will you ever get off the mat?
Oh my fluffy cat
Will you ever get off this mat?

Aisha Khan (9)
Geoffrey Field Junior School, Reading

The Emotion Happy

When I think of happy I think of the colour yellow.
Happy is the colour of ripe bananas on a tree.
Happy is the emotion that I want to be.
Happy makes you smile when you are having fun.
Happy is my emotion when my work is done.
Happy is the best that you can ever be.
Happy, happy, happy,
This is me!
Happy.

Kian Patrick Williams (8)
Geoffrey Field Junior School, Reading

The Strawberry Cake

One day I ate cake.
I went to the forest and I saw a snake.
Then I shook and jumped in the lake.
I was so sad, I felt bad.
I'm going to take my punishment
And read 'Mac the Mouse'
And sit in a sack and lie on my back
And not whack anything for a joke
And I will not play with my cloak.

Mayhnez Sikeder (8)
Geoffrey Field Junior School, Reading

Nightmare Of Reality

D on't panic, it's what I'm telling myself now

A ll around me, I'm trapped, I can't escape

N ever-ending, the panic is never-ending

G ot to get out

E xpecting the worst; I don't know what to do...

R eality... I can't escape the reality.

Lexi-Rose Hickey (8)

Geoffrey Field Junior School, Reading

My Grandad

My grandad is bright,
My grandad is cool,
He's too cool for school,
When I think of him, I sing a little tune,
Grandad in the sky, it's hard to say goodbye,
I really don't know why
But cancer made you die,
I know you like what you can see
And I know you really, really love me.

Lewis Jenkinson (9)
Geoffrey Field Junior School, Reading

8

Pirates, Pirates, Naughty Pirates

Pirates, pirates, naughty pirates,
Stealing every penny,
Not leaving hardly any,
Robbing British merchant ships,
Only leaving a couple of bones and bits.
Going crazy, not being lazy,
You must catch 'em when they do,
'Cause if you don't, they'll catch you!

Finn Bunker (9)
Geoffrey Field Junior School, Reading

Why God Created Teachers

When God created teachers,
He created them so
They could be rock stars.
Mrs Hardacker makes us,
Then she bakes us.
My teacher is really,
Lovely, caring, helpful.
The class really loves her.
She helps us learn.
She helps us turn.

Daisy Maze (8)
Geoffrey Field Junior School, Reading

Sand, Sun And A Book

Sand is yellow, sand is white,
Sky is blue, sky is white.
Water's blue, water's white.
Books are heavy, books are light.
Water's big, water's light.
Sun is high, sun is near,
Sun is good, sun is bad.

Shawaiz Mirza (8)
Geoffrey Field Junior School, Reading

Emotions

(A diamante poem)

Sorrow,
Unhappy, hopeless,
Disappointing, disgusting, depressing,
Low, glory, pleasant, bright,
Encouraging, existing, uplifting,
Happy, cheerful,
Joy.

Alina Majid (8)
Geoffrey Field Junior School, Reading

A Cake

Cake, bake, ready to make.
Mix! Mix! Mix! Mix the ingredients.
Cake make, bake, ready to cook,
Take it out and cut it up.
Now it's ready to be served.

Millie Grace Williams (8)

Geoffrey Field Junior School, Reading

Britain

Winston Churchill, William Shakespeare,
Jessica Ennis, Idris Elba, Mo Farah.
William Shakespeare, can't you see
British skies are grey?
Bright countryside is green.
As for British skin colour,
There are thousands I've seen.
There are just three British colours that should
matter to you
And the famous oh so very British red, white and
blue.
The tea 'n' scones, Ant 'n' Dec.
One Direction, Will 'n' Kate.
British trains they'll make you late.
Simon Cowell, Posh 'n' Becks, fish 'n' chips.
Alesha Dixon, famous Brits include Adele,
Alexander Graham Bell.
We invented everything from the telly to the Web.
We gave the world football
And we love a good celeb.
We watch them in the jungle,
To Ant 'n' Dec they beg.

We prefer Amanda Holden to someone like Nick Clegg.
Traditional dish is vindaloo.
We beat the French at Waterloo.
Tesco and Poundland,
Plumbers from all the land.
Next time you see another Union Jack,
Think what this country's given you
Then try to give some back.
Tolerance and acceptance for Muslim, Sikh or Jew.
I'm so proud, oh so proud of this red, white and blue.
Grey skies, sleet 'n' snow,
Politicians on the make,
Winter virus, flu outbreak,
never sun, only rain,
Our favourite thing is to complain,
But none of that should get you down.
Never ever get you down
Because this is Britain,
All of our Britain, home of the crown!

Nailah Nazar (10)
Iqra Slough Islamic Primary School, Fernside

Haunted House

I was walking normally in the moonlight
But when I turned my head around
I saw something in the dark night,
A spooky house, dark grey stone,
Then I imagined some
Fraying carpets and mummies' moans,
I made a very bad decision
And decided to enter.

Creaking floorboards, flying bats,
Weird objects, for example; hats,
Crawling spiders, cobwebs many,
Ordinary people, there isn't any!
Ancient paintings, creepy tombs,
The gigantic towers seem to loom.
I think there's something moving,
over by that chair,
But when I take a closer look,
There is really nothing there!

I think it is time for me to go,
Before all the lights over there,
Start to glow.
I ran out of this place
And tried to get out
And I surely know
I am not coming back here again!

Mashal Baig (11)
Iqra Slough Islamic Primary School, Fernside

The Best Excuses

I had started on my homework
But I spilt my tasty drink.
My dog ate my homework
And then the pen ran out of ink.

I accidentally dropped it
On my disgusting dog's poopings.
My sister flushed it down the toilet,
When I wasn't looking.

My mother washed my homework
In the washer and dryer.
It was next to a socket
And it caught on fire.

Hurricanes blew my notes away,
Lightning struck our town,
My homework was taken away
By an evil killer clown.

I worked so hard on these excuses,
I read and read and read,

Then my teacher asked,
'Did you do this in bed?'

Yasmeen Yousuf (9)

Iqra Slough Islamic Primary School, Fernside

Time

When the sun leaps out from its hiding,
The birds start to tweet,
Not a melancholy thing in sight,
The animals wake up and have their morning feast.
When we decide to wake up
The animals start doing their daily jobs.
And when we finish breakfast
It's their lunchtime. Suddenly, everyone stops,
When we walk to school, the sun says, 'Hello.'
The animals are finished and start to head home
And we are just listening to the teacher drone.
It's our lunchtime and the animals go to bed,
We have one hour to play and refresh our heads.
It's our home time, we are happy to see our mums,
We have our supper and then the day is done.

Nusayba Yusuf (10)
Iqra Slough Islamic Primary School, Fernside

Dream Guess

I come to you really slow, but go fast
To happily have me, you must forget the past.
I can only breathe under your air,
Striving for me, life gets pretty tough,
So you need to be fair,
They who have me are stars,
Stars that can't shine without darkness.
You need to be ready to fight,
A major thing you need to know,
If you want your light to show...
Be you,
Love you,
Make sure you are your complete self.
I am like the sun for you,
If you cover me, it will be dark,
You won't see the true,
You'd have to live in a scary closet,
If you don't try to achieve...
Your beautiful, lovely dream!

Hiba Kaunain Ali (10)

Iqra Slough Islamic Primary School, Fernside

Ice Cream Dream

When I have a little taste
Of the best thing ever,
It's melting in my mouth,
Just the perfect weather
For ice cream!

So many different flavours to choose from,
Vanilla, strawberry, chocolate, bubblegum,
It's way better than milkshakes
And yummier than cheesecakes!

As soon as you hear the ice cream truck,
Nog your mum for a buck,
Race to the road before it's too late,
Yum, yum, yum... doesn't it taste great?

Ice cream is mine and your favourite!
Now you can try it with different toppings,
Nuts, sprinkles, fruit and hot fudge.
Mmm... palatable!

Fatima Ahmed (10)
Iqra Slough Islamic Primary School, Fernside

Stars

In the velvet, pitch-dark night,
You are shining very bright,
I still remember you twinkle, twinkle,
You are peeping in the window,
A molecule of the moon,
From here you look like a tiny spoon.

When I'm thinking of you,
You are becoming brighter.
When I'm looking sad
I think of you and I become mightier.
I'm sleeping, you wake up playing with the moon.
As I wake up, I say goodnight
To the cheerful, white, glistening moon.

As I still remember you twinkle, twinkle all the
night,
In the velvet, pitch-dark night.
You are shining very bright.

Madiha Hashmi (8)
Iqra Slough Islamic Primary School, Fernside

Ghostown

Ghostown, Ghostown where are you?
I have been looking for you,
Years and months have passed,
I remember the shivers go down my spine,
When the lights used to flicker behind,
I am walking everywhere looking for you,
Trying to find a sign
That directs me to you,
When the mummies pop out of nowhere,
I remember screaming, 'Go away.'
I remember the flying bats,
Dark as black cats,
Now I am as sad as a rat
And need someone to help.
All I need to do is go to my friend,
Ghostown, there you are,
You have been behind me for the last year.

Muhammad Jalal Baig (8)
Iqra Slough Islamic Primary School, Fernside

Miraculous Mum

My mum, my miraculous mum
Is as bright as the sun.
So bright,
She is my light.
My smiling diamond in the night.
My mum, my mum,
So pretty; never glum.
Flies through life,
Never sleeps in the night.
I will never let her go,
Always fast, never slow.
My mum, my miraculous mum
Is as bright as the sun.
In my dreams there she comes.
A blanket of kindness, wrapped around me.
I can't control my body when she is anywhere else.
Her love for me weighs one thousand tonnes.
Life is amazing when you have a miraculous mum!

Eisha Ahmed (10)
Iqra Slough Islamic Primary School, Fernside

Googlies And Me

Creepers, creepers everywhere,
Can you believe we breathe the same air?
Zombies tear your doors down,
They'll make you run right out of town.

Endermen are everywhere,
They're so scary they'll make you pull out your hair.
Spiders will never ever eat in the day,
Their favourite colour is grey.

One day I was mining for one,
I was going to find something for sure.
What's that shiny blue one?
I mined some diamonds, not one but more.
A googly snuck up behind me
And I was there no more!

Zeenath Riffky
Iqra Slough Islamic Primary School, Fernside

Stopping By The Wood On A Cold Day

Whose woods are these?
I think I know.
His house is in the village though.
He will not see me stopping here
To watch his woods fill up with snow.

My little horse must think it queer,
To stop without a farmhouse near.
Between the woods and frozen lake,
The darkest evening of the year.

The woods are lovely, dark and deep,
But I have a promise to keep,
I just have to leap
And miles to go before I sleep.

Amtul Syeda
Iqra Slough Islamic Primary School, Fernside

The Hunt!

Creeping and crawling,
Ready to slay,
Steadily waiting
To eat his prey.

Saliva dripping,
Looking to feast,
Prowling and stalking,
A wildebeest!

His claws sharp like knives,
His glossy fur,
Sparkling as he dives,
Fast as a blur.

Running then jumping,
At the horned brute,
Growling and fighting
To get his loot.

Strolling to his plain,
Filled with his lunch,

Shaking his huge mane,
What's next to munch?

Khadeejah Zamir (8)

Iqra Slough Islamic Primary School, Fernside

Parents

Mother and Father love me so,
What if I woke up one day
And saw that I was all alone?

If your parents are with you,
It would be a dream come true.

They would cherish you,
Love you and never let you go.

Imagine an empty life
With no role model.

Who would you have then?
Who would support you?
Who would love you?

Without this blessing
You would have a miserable life.

Khuzamah Bibi (9)
Iqra Slough Islamic Primary School, Fernside

Everyday Life

Exploring new worlds,
Pickaxe I'm in need.
New mobs roaming around,
Defeated with plain ease.

Returning back home
Tired!
Back to bed,
Morning again,
Sword let's slaughter some sheep.

Run, run, I've found a treat,
Defeated a skeleton,
Tamed Amy (the wolf).

Night has come,
Zombies growling,
Painful death, by daylight power!

Saleema Khan (9)
Iqra Slough Islamic Primary School, Fernside

The Rainforest

R ainy, wet days
A nimals of different sizes
I rresistible, cute mammals
N ever too little life
F eel the warmth of the forest
O xygen we receive
R eptiles of many kinds
E ndangered species
S ounds that are peaceful and wonderful
T errible deforestation
S ave the rainforest!

Salma Sana (9)
Iqra Slough Islamic Primary School, Fernside

Cool Dog

One sunny day, on my way home,
I found a dog and said, 'Don't moan.'
The dog was so cool,
I couldn't believe she came to school.
She was so happy,
I named her Gabby.
I put her in my pocket,
One ate my Lockets.
When she saw my mum,
Her face looked like a plum,
She ran like a cheetah
And she was scared of my teacher.

Muneeb Shafqaat (8)
Iqra Slough Islamic Primary School, Fernside

Glad To Be Me

I am proud to be me.
I am good in my own ways.
I am bad in my own ways
But I am still me.
I may be happy.
I may be sad
But I'm still me.
There is no one I'd rather be
Than me!
No one looks like me.
No one talks like me.
No one walks like me.
No one says the same things as me.
I am unique.
I am me.

Hannah Baig (10)
Iqra Slough Islamic Primary School, Fernside

Nature

Spring comes only once a year,
The birds chirping loudly for all of us to hear.

Summer will soon arrive,
The sun shines and charming flowers arise.

Autumn brings the changing of the leaves,
Pretty colours falling from the wooden trees.

Poor dead leaves are found,
Snow is piling up on the frozen ground.

Fatima Azeem (10)
Iqra Slough Islamic Primary School, Fernside

Under The Sea!

Beneath the ocean
Wavy and cool
The mermaids keep
A dancing school.

The oysters jog
The lobsters prance
The dolphins come
To join the dance.

The jellyfish
Who are rather small
Never know the steps at all!

Fatima Shafqaat
Iqra Slough Islamic Primary School, Fernside

Family

We laugh
We cry
Arguing and then
Wondering why.
We give
We love
We act tough
Separate we're weak
Together we're family.

Haleema Haqeeq Dar (10)
Iqra Slough Islamic Primary School, Fernside

Mobs

There is a walking bomb
And it's ticking along,
A teleporting man
Is called an Enderman,
Kill him with anything except a block if you can,
Like something was going to go wrong,
I found a pig and a cow,
As I dug down,
I found a witch,
That made me twitch,
I didn't wait to bow down,
I set off and found a sheep
That was close to a river that was deep,
A zombie villager, made me shiver
And I ate some sheep meat,
There was a glitch
And there was another witch,
I found something big
And it was a pig,
Then I saw a lever switch,
I saw a squid and stole its ink,

I saw a blaze,
While in a Minecraft maze,
Oh my goodness, this is the best game in the
world...
I think.

Erinn Rose (10)
Manor Primary School, Reading

Items

This is a poem about the items in Minecraft,
Listen carefully as this is my Rhymecraft.
First you need a weapon,
Just in case you come face-to-face with the
Ender Dragon.
You'll never find the dragon in a mineshaft,
If you do, select your sword and chop him in half.

If you see a skeleton, take his bow,
But make sure that you know
That it won't kill as much as an enchanted
diamond sword,
However you might go and kill a couple of cows
Or pigs if you're bored.

Another item is a pickaxe,
They are really good at defending enemy attacks,
The spear is also good for creepers that come too
near.
Whatever you choose...
Pick wisely, because you want to make sure that
you don't lose.

Delphine Georgette Lindo (11)

Manor Primary School, Reading

My Minecraft Life

Here in Minecraft
I'm sitting in a mineshaft.
There is a pig
Who ate some figs.
This is my life in Minecraft.

I woke up from my bed
With my cat on my head.
I ate some delicious cheese
And then I sneezed.
Oh wait! My cat hasn't been fed.

In my section there were blocks,
Some of them were ticking clocks.
Now I am going to bake,
I am going to make a cake.
The cakes are one of my favourite blocks.

When I was digging, I found some gold,
Behold the weapon that made me bold.
Then I was looking at my friends,
They were looking at flower stems.
I'm the queen of finding gold, so behold!

L'shae Perkins (9)
Manor Primary School, Reading

My Minecraft World!

Minecraft,
I love this game,
Although it's addictive,
It's definitely not lame,
Rhymecraft.

Let me tell you a little bit about it...
The square sky cried
And the mooshroom cow lied.
The chicken died
And the horse took a ride.

Then it took a million years,
I was full of fears
But then I did it,
The TNT as a firework on the ground,
It made a thunderous sound.

Did you know...?
The horse came back,
The mooshroom was in a sack,
The chicken lied,
He wasn't really dead,

But the sky still cried
Because he thought the chicken was in bed.

Naajidah Muminah (11)
Manor Primary School, Reading

Places, Places

Tell me how to play Minecraft
The animals, biomes and places.
Tell me how to get to a mineshaft,
How you can even create horse races?

Wolves, wolves everywhere
But beware, other mobs are around.
Give a wolf a bone but it won't share,
Be careful, be careful as the creepers make no
sound.

The Nether is the Minecraft hell,
Steve be careful, the lava is smoking.
Oh yes, that rings a bell,
That fortress over there, I'm really not joking.

I'm going to mine some iron
That shines as bright as the sun,
But instead, I found a new biome
And soon I was having lots of fun.

Niamh Curtis (10)
Manor Primary School, Reading

My Minecraft Day!

Fighting like a dragon in the night,
Makes me feel delight
And shine bright in the light.

The sword is in action,
This makes a wonderful reaction.
When it slices off their heads,
I can finally go back to bed.

The sky cried
And the lightning struck.
When the zombies killed
I felt like I'd been hit by a truck.

Wondering and wondering all day long
Has made my dog into a log.
The mobs are like a deathtrap,
They are very hard to find on a map.
The chest groaned when I put my staff in it,
When I take my weapons out of it
I'm ready to be hit.

Jane Kamara (10)
Manor Primary School, Reading

Weapons!

Axe as sharp as a knife!
Mining for your life.
If you stop, you will pop.
Then you will respawn,
Get a diamond sword before you get bored.
Zombies come, time to fight,
Now let's go find some pigs.
Dig, dig, dig,
Still no pig,
But you still found gold.
Now you think you're rich
But a witch stole your gold,
Now you just got fooled,
You found a witch,
Then you dialled,
She got fooled.
Now you rule
And go and find a boss.
You get up,
Killing time to go home.

Now you've had some fun
Our day is done.
We hope you have some fun!

Ross Junior Kelly (10)
Manor Primary School, Reading

My Minecraft Life

I make a pool
'Cause Herobrine is cruel.
Blocks, blocks, so many blocks.
I wish to create a rock,
I have many tools.

Mobs are creatures that can kill,
I need to write an important will.
Houses are made out of bricks,
To make a wooden sword you need some sticks.
I hate creepers still.

Minecraft is a game.
The zombie is my name.
I get eggs every day.
I like to go and stay
Like a cat I can tame.

Creative is cool,
Notch does rule.
Creepers are terrifying,
Oh I hate it, when they start sizzling.
I am small.

Omer Richard Kaymak (9)
Manor Primary School, Reading

Steve And Minecraft...

This is a story about Minecraft and Steve,
There are blocks, items, food and myths that make
you believe,
Dig, dig, dig you'll reach the lava,
Unless you can fly, this will be a disaster,
Remember the objective is to make Steve achieve,
However, nothing built can last forever,
You'll only survive if you are clever,
The easiest weapon to get is a sword,
While playing Minecraft, it's very hard to get bored,
Also, I bet you'll never get a skull-bone
And a creeper together,
I do know one thing though
Me and Minecraft go together like birds of a
feather.

Alan Lucas (10)

Manor Primary School, Reading

Minecraft Raining

There was Steve
And he took me to his lair.
Then he told me to leave
But I started to stare.

In sight there was a mine
And there was a bone
But he ran out of time
So he quickly gathered some stone.

The next day there were diamonds,
It was a race.
It was like a diamond island,
Then I went back to base.

There was a bed
But it was in sight
And it was red
Then it turned to night.

Then I saw Alex,
Then I said, 'Hi.'

She took me to her palace
Then I started to die.

Kiala Gittens (9)
Manor Primary School, Reading

Minecraft Wolves

Wolves are very kind
If you tame them in time.
They are grey in their eyes
Be careful, they bite.

They have grey fur
Oh no, he's going to bite her!
I have to stroke her
Now she is as gentle as a dove bird.

If you attack them they bite
So get your sword and fight.
They win, you're a kite
Run away, they gave a fright.

You get an axe
Trap them in a sack.
'Yay,' you've trapped the wolf pack
The sack kicks, you trip
You let the wolves go, they attack.

Danny Rutabingwa (9)
Manor Primary School, Reading

Missions

This is a rhyme all about Minecraft,
In fact I guess you could call this one Rhymecraft.
Why, you ask?
My teacher set me this task about a game,
To write a poem
About how when you play Minecraft
It's never the same.
Defeating the Ender Dragon is a quest,
Remember it won't be easy, it will be a test.
Defeat the Wither and you will be at the end,
If you're brave, you will click start and play again.
A quick tip before I go...
There's more information on the Minecraft website
If you want to know.

Lily Scott (10)
Manor Primary School, Reading

Mia-Rae's Minecraft Poem

One day I saw a sheep
On a hill that was very steep.
Then I set the sheep on fire,
As I walked towards it, the flames got higher.
The sheep fell in a hole that was deep.

The next day, I decided to make
But then I fell in a lake.
Next to that, I saw a sheep
Who was in a hay heap,
Maybe I should go somewhere else to make.

Then I was on my way
To a place the very next day.
I didn't mind where I went
As long as nothing was bent
And there wasn't sheep in hay.

Mia-Rae Lucas (10)
Manor Primary School, Reading

Minecraft World

M inecraft is a place where monsters come to life

I n a haunted house, there's a zombie with a knife

N ever get pushed by a creeper or it will explode near your home

E very day, look for torches so monsters don't go near your gold

C raft swords to fight monsters

R espect your dog so it will fight with you

A little cat, walking across a bridge with a little fish

F ighting monsters with gold swords

T he sun is going down, I start to shiver like a cloud.

Shanyce-Renay (9)

Manor Primary School, Reading

Marley's Minecraft Sonnet

There was a race with a ghast
Plus a skeleton who was first
The ghast was very last
And the skeleton was about to burst.

Oh no Herobrine's free
Let's escape
Now's my time to flee
Plus I ran with a cape.

Now let's talk about the End
There are Endermen
Let me just say the End really needs a mend
Yeah Enderman are just like a lamb.

I searched and searched and saw a diamond sea
Herobrine found me, he's looking at me!

Marley Dalfsen (9)
Manor Primary School, Reading

Minecraft

M inecraft, you have to be careful everywhere you go in the night

I n Minecraft, you can make your own house

N ow you can get a pet mouse

E ndermen look as dark as the midnight sky

C reepers look as green as grass right in front of you

R un when a zombie is following you, run for your life!

A fter you have done, make the light come upon you

F ield's open, you go and explore your life

T each your friends how to play Minecraft as well.

Darcey Antwi (9)
Manor Primary School, Reading

Building The House

Bricks, they are tougher than sticks,
As nice as a rose
And bigger than your nose.
So when you build a house
Sticks are the way to go.

Foundation, it's not a reincarnation.
It holds the decoration.
Also it's where the house is
And it's where no mouse will go,
Not in a million years.

Glass
As clear as a class.
It keeps the mobs visible
Rather than invisible
And the glass is a shield,
Also they are lots of shades.

Vinnie Johnson (11)
Manor Primary School, Reading

A Cinquain About Minecraft

In Minecraft I tried to escape from Herobrine
While searching for a horse
And that's when I heard the clock chime
Then I saw a circular source.

Here comes Enderman, I lost my health
I dug and dug then saw diamonds
I sadly lost my wealth
The mountains stare as Steve weaves between islands.

I looked deeper and saw the diamond sun
I grabbed my weapons
When I died because of Enderman, it wasn't fun
Was I in the Nether or in the heavens?

Elisha Binama (9)
Manor Primary School, Reading

Minecraft

M inecraft is a game that you would think is lame

I 'm in love with the game

N ever look in an Enderman's eye, because they will make you die

E nd is where you kill the Ender Dragon

C reepers are lions, running to bed at night

R unning as fast as you can from zombies

A day has just ended, but there is still much more to find

F ood helps you to survive

T ry not to die when the sun goes down.

Keeleigh O'Reilly (10)
Manor Primary School, Reading

The Life Of Minecraft

My name is Steve, I am a boy
I really want a large toy
I have a lot of boy pets
One of them had to go to the vet.

One day, it passed away
Now all I want to do is stay
Then I found a diamond
But I met a guy called Simon.

He likes to get gold
That he likes to hold
He likes to eat sheep
While I'm digging deep.

I found a new friend
His name is Ken
He loves lots of hens.

Jayden Charlie Williams (9)
Manor Primary School, Reading

My Minecraft Wish!

Before it was Eve,
I saw Steve,
Riding in a mine cart
On his way to Minecraft.

I tried to run,
But I was outdone.
It was nearly Christmas
And I thought my wish had come.
The sky was night
And it was bright.

I still wish I was a character,
So I walked until I reached a cave,
To claim something that I have saved.
I've come to kill my little Dave
That I named... the Ender Dragon.

Tamar Sesay (10)
Manor Primary School, Reading

Minecraft

M ine and build a house with a bed

I f you don't eat, you will end up dead

N ever stop playing, play all day, all night

E ndermen's eyes are dogs searching for meat

C an't stop even if I see a creeper

R owing in the sea with my boat

A fter a super long trip I like to eat apples

F ind a fishing rod and try to get fish

T he zombies are like slugs crawling to their home.

Jayden Harris-Shute (9)

Manor Primary School, Reading

My Minecraft Poem

M ine in the day, not in the night

 I f you do, creepers will give you a fright

N ever give up, you will get there one day

E ndermen are slugs that never say, 'Hey'

C rafting all day is like rowing a boat

R aking all day I wish I had a goat

A fter I sleep, I get out of bed

F ighting all day, it's hurting my head

T he Wither is strong, I wish I could beat it.

Aydan Cole (9)

Manor Primary School, Reading

A Creeper

A creeper is a monster
That will give you a fright.
They're scared in the day
And come out at night.
You would know when they're near
By the sound you can hear.
Don't ever let them inside,
Otherwise a message will pop up
Saying, 'Steve's died'.
Watch out, the creepers will explode
Right where you just hoed.
Although you will try to have fun
The creepers will always make you run.

Charlotte Freeman (10)
Manor Primary School, Reading

Minecraft Poem

M ops are in your inventory

I ce might be outside if it's cold

N asty because you will turn gold

E ndermen are black shadows that pick up blocks

C hests are always in a village house

R ats might step on your laptop or mouse

A wesome arrows can kill animals for your food

F eed your pets every day to stay healthy

T raps won't work on you if you are a character.

Taleen Abzuberre (9)
Manor Primary School, Reading

Abidur-Rahman's Quatrain About Minecraft

Hey, do you like playing Minecraft?
I had to die because of Herobrine.
Have you seen a mineshaft?
That was when the clock chimed.

You know you need to survive,
I go to many schools,
Make your armour look alive,
I use jewels to make a lot of tools.

As quick as a cheetah,
I traded with some villagers.
I made a good deal,
This is a good game for teenagers,
It seems really real.

Abidur-Rahman Chowdhury (9)
Manor Primary School, Reading

Untitled

This is a story all about how
Steve found a diamond
But then he flipped upside down.

But Steve heard a sound
That made him quickly turn around.
What he saw made him pull out his sword.
Then he went on to find something that blew his mind.

I'm gonna fight because I need a light,
Despite my broken sword, ouch,
I've been hurt, I'm bleeding,
Now I'm dead.

Alex James Heath (11)
Manor Primary School, Reading

I Craft On Minecraft We All Craft

M inecraft is the best game you can play

 I t's the best I can name

N othing is better than this game

 E ndermen are as spooky as dragons

 C hests are always in the village

R un, run, make sure you're as quiet as a mouse

A nd always be ready for creepers there

 F ind weapons so you can defeat the zombies

T errifying zombies are coming for you!

Amie Samba (9)

Manor Primary School, Reading

A Deal Of Life

A lovely day in Minecraft
You need to mine into a mineshaft.
Sleeping on a bed,
Getting a skeleton head.
His dream has finally come,
His mission is done.
Finding a deal,
What a great meal.
Mining some coal,
Trapped in a hole.
Getting out of the hole,
Eating soup into a bowl.
My hunger bar is full,
Now I need some wool.
Chopping some wood.
Oh wow! This game is good.

Ali Mohamed Mekiri (10)

Manor Primary School, Reading

Minecraft

M ining brick by brick

I cy place don't slip

N ever give up, push yourself forward

E ndermen are scary, they will kill you

C rafting is a fun thing to do

R espawn yourself, don't die every time

A t last you will get sleepy so get a bed

F inally, get a knife and go through the night

T hen you eat your tea which is meat, then go to sleep.

Katie Fidler (9)

Manor Primary School, Reading

Minecraft Is A Game

M inecraft is a game I play

I hope that tomorrow is a better day

N o one wants the square sky to cry

E veryone has a chance to die

C haracters are a picture

R hymecraft is a competition

A ll of the people know that Rhymecraft is cool

F orever they think about adding a pool

T hinking that Minecraft is like family to Rhymecraft.

Georgia Fairchild (10)

Manor Primary School, Reading

Minecraft Power

M ake a house of your own

I n the forest throw the wolves a bone

N ever go out at night

E very day is a quest

C reepers are as dangerous as a hungry shark

R espawn next to your house to save your life

A fter you throw a bone to a wolf, it is your pet

F or treasure, open a chest

T unnels are helpful, so is your sword.

Rubi Loughnane (10)
Manor Primary School, Reading

Minecraft

M aking houses and mining ore

I f a zombie breaks your door

N ever run away or you're dead

E ndermen are black clouds that will steal your blocks

C reepers are like worms crawling to a leaf

R ich as ever as a survivor

A mazing people are mining too

F ixing bases just like you

T he best game ever is Minecraft!

Jayden Fry (9)
Manor Primary School, Reading

The Ender Dragon

There was once a man called Steve
Who was very pleased
And he had a dream to kill a creeper
Who people believe, teased if you achieved.
Then you will get a diamond, set of keys,
Now with these keys
You can weave things together
Like a key to the weather.
Now I am ready to kill the Ender Dragon,
Now you go and grab the egg
And go and kill the Wither.

Matthew Cox (10)
Manor Primary School, Reading

A Miner's Journey

M ining, making a path

I n a massive mineshaft

N othing built can last forever

E verything I built was blown up by a creeper

C an the diamond not be blown away?

R uined to bits, I hope it stays!

A nd stolen by the lava

F ell and burned, what a disaster!

T hat didn't happen, the diamond stayed, hooray!

Kiera Peacock (10)

Manor Primary School, Reading

Weapons

(A cinquain poem)

Get set
And load your bow,
Aim and shoot some creepers,
Run away before they explode,
You won.

Cut them,
Zombies will die,
Then go and find some more,
Kill some pigs so that you can eat,
Enjoy.

Go home,
It is night-time,
Take care and stay alert,
Or grab your sword and slay some mobs,
Be brave.

Kiran Acharya (10)
Manor Primary School, Reading

My Life

Digging in the dusk, which is like a maze,
Mine through the night,
Keep a watch,
Creepers are in sight.

Find a smile of Ender,
A sneaky sound in the Nether,
Mooshroom-covered cow mob,
Dropping beef or leather.

Creepers! Creepers!
Don't come this way,
Build yourself a fortress,
I know I'm your prey.

Reema Muhajireen (10)
Manor Primary School, Reading

The Creeper

There was once a creeper,
That would give you a fright.
If he came near, the end would be here.
Every time he exploded he would get lava coated.
It was diamond and gold, that he would hold.
Just in case, if you come face-to-face,
With such a disgrace,
Swing out your sword
And if you're lucky,
You might just become the next lord.

Shivani Gurung (10)
Manor Primary School, Reading

Minecraft Is A Great Game

M inecraft is a great game

I n the game, we all play the same

N ext day the square sky will cry

E veryone thinks when you sleep, it is like you die

C haracters are dragons

R hymecraft is the best

A nd we make a nest

F illing in blocks to finish a build

T hinking of a Minecraft house.

Jorja Evans (10)
Manor Primary School, Reading

Minecraft

M inecraft is a brilliant game to play

I like to go to the sea to get some hay

N aughty creepers come out to play

E ndermen are a lion's roar

C hest keeps your blocks safe

R ivers are deep

A nimals can be ridden

F erns cook your food nicely

T NT explodes lots of blocks.

Danny Mark Eaton (9)

Manor Primary School, Reading

Minecraft

M inecraft is an awesome game to play

I could play it all day

N ever giving up

E ndermen chasing us with swiftness like a cheetah

C rafting till the end as a team

R iding on mine carts

A lways mining for diamonds

F inding lots of caves

T emples are everywhere in the sand biome.

Navarro Graham (9)

Manor Primary School, Reading

Jasmita's Minecraft Poem

M inecraft is not lame

I really love this game

N ow I know the most powerful weapon is a sword

E nder Dragon, all hail, is the lord

C rafting is as cool as ice

R iding and jumping onto the rocks

A xes can be let loose

F illing houses with blocks

T he sword is a tiger tooth.

Jasmita Sehra (10)
Manor Primary School, Reading

Minecraft

Building with bricks all day,
Making houses.
The brick is blue like the sea,
The house is beautiful to me.

Zombies are creepy
And they are freaky.

I don't want to see zombies,
But they want to see me.

Minecraft is a game,
I played it with my mate,
I loved it when I played.

Urwa Nazir (10)
Manor Primary School, Reading

Creepers Are Weird

C reepers are weird,

R egeneration gets me into fire,

E ndermen are as black as night,

E ven though I don't see them loads,

P laying the game gets me on the go,

E ndermen also get me on a boat,

R hymecraft is the best,

S ometimes the Ender Dragon is a pest.

Ryan Smith (11)
Manor Primary School, Reading

The Weapons

Shoot it
At enemies.
Shoot it at evil mobs.
Pull it back hard, aim and shoot.
Then win.
Cut mops or
Massive trees.
Cut down the enemy
With his useful item,
Survive all day.
It's sharp to kill players.
It's strong so it won't break.
Kill every evil player,
Be tough.

Kai Furnivall (10)
Manor Primary School, Reading

Minecraft

M ake a house of your own

I n Minecraft zombies like to moan

N ight goes on and on

E nder in the dark monsters

C reepers are like green grass

R oses are red, violets are blue, be careful zombies

A re coming for you

F lying creatures

T NT can blow up.

Mason James Hale-Cox (9)

Manor Primary School, Reading

Minecraft

M inecraft is cool

I f you don't play it you're a fool

N ever will I ever

E nd up at the Nether

C ried in the night

R emember I'm a nightmare

A nd I made it through the night

F or all of your delight

T hen I played Minecraft again.

Dylan Hancock (10)

Manor Primary School, Reading

Minecraft Isn't Lame

(Haiku and cinquain poems)

Minecraft is a game,
But that doesn't mean I'm lame,
Steve looks like a block.

Minecraft
Makes me sleepy,
Only when I'm weepy.
The red lava is a death pool,
Rhymecraft.

Minecraft runs my days,
It shouts at me when I lay,
In my Minecraft bed.

Rayann Maliuna (10)
Manor Primary School, Reading

Diamond Adventure

If you are brave and plucky,
Plus, of course, you have to be lucky,
You may find shining diamonds,
Not forgetting green emeralds,
Be careful,
Beware,
Don't dig straight down,
Who knows what's there?
It's love you need to find
And diamonds won't be far behind.

Ayrton David Stewart (11)
Manor Primary School, Reading

Minecraft

M inecraft is a game

I t's not that lame

N ether is a place

E nchanted by a face

C ringy like a creeper

R emember, it's not a good sleeper

A nd it's a skyscraper

F ound some lava

T hen spawned a llama.

Keyessence Montaque (10)

Manor Primary School, Reading

Evil Mobs

Skeletons are cool
They shoot people like you
They burn in the sun too.

Creepers are monsters
And they live in dumpsters.
He had a head as green as grass
And I would pass.

Endermen are cool
They pick up blocks for you
They teleport too.

Alannah Louise White (10)
Manor Primary School, Reading

Deadly Weapons

Axe as sharp as a knife,
Mining through your life.
If you stop, you can respond
You would have your bomb
Pulling out your sword
To stop you getting bored.
You can kill a mob
And have some fun,
But only when you run
So don't be dumb,
Enjoy the fun.

Kevin Tuleassi (10)
Manor Primary School, Reading

Minecraft

Minecraft is a game
I get insane when I play
And it really makes my day.

Creepers are smelly
They growl like my belly
Their brains are jelly
And they like to eat berries.

Potions are cool
But if you use them wrong, you will be a fool.

Ela Erceri (10)
Manor Primary School, Reading

Ledlie's Minecraft

Minecraft
Adventurous, constructive
Building, creating, axing
Minecraft is exciting
It can be confusing, petrifying
Minecraft.

Creeper
Scary, ferocious
Sizzling, frightening, exploding
He can be vicious, destructive
Creeper.

Ledlie George-Kwaku Otu (9)
Manor Primary School, Reading

Minecraft

B lock and a lock
L ook for a block
O ver the door
C all for creepers
K eep your doors shut tight
S melly creepers creeping like zombies in the night.

Ellie-Rose Barnes (10)

Manor Primary School, Reading

Fruit

Lemons are sour,
Lemons aren't sweet,
Lemon peelings at my feet.

Strawberries are delicious,
Strawberries are sweet,
I'm making up a fruity beat.

Bananas are yellow,
Bananas are long,
I've got a banana microphone for this song.

Mangos are ripe,
Mangos are smooth,
Mangos make me want to groove.

Grapes are green,
Grapes are red,
Grapes are going round in my head.

Here is my fruit melody,
I've mixed it with a spoon,
Now I've got a perfect tune.

Ella Weaving (7)
Oldfield Primary School, Maidenhead

Liar

At first I thought I could trust you,
But clearly I was wrong.
You could have chosen your own path,
Yet you chose to join the throng.

To me you had meant everything
But the truth was soon found out.
You lied to me in person,
Of that, I had no doubt.

How can I trust somebody
Who'll lie and lie and lie?
Who won't work when they're told to,
Why you barely even try!

Let's face it, you're a liar,
You don't deserve my trust.
So I will keep away from you,
I will because I must.

You lied to me in person,
Now that is just not fair.
You had better apologise quickly,
For I'm madder than a bear!

Oliver Green (10)
Oldfield Primary School, Maidenhead

An Autumn Cliff

Standing at the edge
Of a cliff looking down.
All of the trees
Wearing leaves like a gown.

A rainbow of colours,
Red, yellow, orange and gold.
Their leaves shining in the sunlight,
Standing out bold.

The wind in my hair,
Whipping my face,
Swirling and twirling,
As if having a race.

Just down below me,
Each leaf has its place,
A carpet of colours
As if made of lace.

The smell of smoke
Rushes up my nose,

As the sun starts to set
And the day comes to a close.

Isabelle Gorf (10)

Oldfield Primary School, Maidenhead

The Race

He had his ears flattened,
He had his nostrils flared,
The only word describing him,
Was totally prepared.

The jockey on his back
Wearing crimson, white and gold,
But little did the rider know
His horse was feeling bold.

He was throwing up his head
And his flanks were heaving.
He wished he was in the gate ready to be leaving.

Bang! went the starting gun
As they galloped off towards the sun.
Horses' hooves thudding on the ground,
The muffled drumming the only sound.

Nina Jasmine Harris (10)
Oldfield Primary School, Maidenhead

Birthday

My birthday's on the 10th of April,
It was really quite a day.
I wore silver heels with funky wheels
And had a great day.

My dress was really sparkly,
It shimmered in the light.
It dazzled so much that it
Blinded people in sight.

We danced until midnight
And had some party food.
We slept in nice comfy beds
And put make-up on too.

I woke up in the morning
Saying goodbye to all my friends.
I felt a bit sad, but it's good,
I'll see them all again.

Jaya Doshi (9)
Oldfield Primary School, Maidenhead

The Little Things In Life

A flower on the breeze,
Some cookies in the tin,
That little hurried feeling,
Before the tide comes in.

A clock that goes tick-tock,
A picture on the wall,
That little, little something,
That you can't just ignore.

A little pot of paint,
That's lying in the sun,
A nagging question in our minds,
That's bugging everyone.

In this big, big universe,
I feel so very small,
But this could be a made-up something,
That isn't real at all.

Leah Johnston (10)
Oldfield Primary School, Maidenhead

The British Weather

Our weather is very funny...
Sometimes it is sunny,
Sometimes it is rainy,
Sometimes there is a rainbow in the sky,
Sometimes there is a rainbow in the puddles,
But I do not mind which one!
Running in the puddles,
Splashing in the water,
Maybe bathing in the sun,
I do prefer bathing in the sun, but
When the rain comes down
It ruins my bun!

Eva Johal (7)
Oldfield Primary School, Maidenhead

As Poor As Could Be

He was as poor as could be
And as helpless as ever,
He didn't look healthy
And was as light as a feather.
The wrinkles on his face made him look 82.
Weak, tired and never slept at night.
When I saw him lying on the floor
It really gave me a fright!
So I ran to see if he was alright,
Soon the ambulance took him away,
I really hope he is okay.

Esha Dosanjh (9)
Oldfield Primary School, Maidenhead

Pigs At The Gig

When I went to the gig
I saw loads of pigs,
Singing along to Little Mix,
Gee, there were loads of pigs,
singing along to Little Mix.

When I went to the gig
I saw loads of pigs,
Sitting in the crowd going,
'Go Little Mix.'

After the gig,
I went out with a pig
And for some reason
He was wearing a wig!

Niamh Campbell (9)
Oldfield Primary School, Maidenhead

Whales

If you ever see a whale,
You'll see it's bigger than a snail.
If you ever see a whale,
You'll see it has one gigantic tail.
If you ever see a whale,
You'll see it never leaves a trail.
If you ever see a whale,
You'll see it's not the fastest male.
Oh yes, I would really like to see...
One great big whale.

Ellie Schlotterbeck (8)
Oldfield Primary School, Maidenhead

My Mother

My mother, my friend so dear,
Throughout my life you're always near.
You're amazing that's true,
I like it when I hug you.
No matter how old I become,
I'll always be your little one.
You help me, then I become free,
I love you from head to knee.
My mum does everything for me,
Whatever she cooks is so yummy!

Riyan Hoque (7)
Oldfield Primary School, Maidenhead

Autumn Is Here Now

Millipedes are softly crawling
Through the cool blades of grass,
Autumn is here now.
Autumn, autumn, autumn.
We are harvesting ready for the snowy season,
winter,
Autumn is here now.
Autumn, autumn, autumn.
Apples are falling, falling, falling down to the
ground,
Autumn is here now.
Autumn, autumn, autumn.

Emily A J Wood (7)
Oldfield Primary School, Maidenhead

Crafting A Rhyme

Rhymecraft, Rhymecraft
Craft me a rhyme,
Craft me one until...
It's time!
Do it till you're out of breath,
Keep on working, yes, yes, yes!
No time for stopping, no, no, no.
Craft it, craft it, craft it now.
Rhymecraft, Rhymecraft,
Do it now!

Jasmin Bouri (7)
Oldfield Primary School, Maidenhead

Fire

Fire, fire all around,
Underneath you,
On the ground!
Fire, fire off you go,
Red, orange and yellow.
Run, run all around,
Because there's fire on the ground.
The fire's spreading, oh no!
Fire, fire off you go,
Red, orange and yellow!

Scarlett Storm (7)
Oldfield Primary School, Maidenhead

Hopscotch

H op along and count with me

O ne, two, three

P ick a stone then

S ing with me!

C ount to ten from

O ne, two, three

T hrow the stone

C ounting with me

H opscotch is a game of glee!

Valentina Aurora Prestel (7)
Oldfield Primary School, Maidenhead

Being Seven

Popping popcorn and shimmering unicorns
Stomping rhinos with long horns
Fizzy lemonade and yummy sweets
Lots and lots of special treats.

Books about princesses and jokes that are funny,
Going scootering when it is sunny.
Brave knights with their shields,
Seeing ponies galloping in the fields.
Sleepovers with best friends
Where the fun never ends.

Cute, fluffy bunnies and heavy hippos,
Eating freezing cold Calippos.
Going on a long holiday
Finding treasure on the way.
Sometimes going to bed late
What will it be like when I am eight?

Addison Faux (7)
Our Lady's Preparatory School, Crowthorne

Once I Saw A Unicorn

Once I saw a unicorn
With a beautiful golden horn.
Its fur was as white as snow
And its hair was tied up in a pretty bow.
When it cried its tears were sweets
And candy is all that it eats.
Its smile is the moon shining up in the sky,
It's so amazing you might want to cry.
Its love goes to all around,
Its feet don't just stay firm on the ground.
When it spreads its wings up high
It's like a diamond in the sky.
So if you see a unicorn like this,
Don't forget that moment of bliss!

Maria Clayton
Our Lady's Preparatory School, Crowthorne

Monsters And Aliens

Monsters, monsters everywhere,
Monsters, monsters here to scare,
Monsters don't like cuddles or hugs,
Monsters are here to suck your blood.

Aliens, aliens they live in space,
Aliens come down to our place,
Aliens won't live in peace,
Aliens want a human feast.

Humans, humans brown, white and black,
Humans together to push the threat back,
Protecting the Earth, protecting each other,
Monsters and aliens should never bother.

Jacob Clay (7)
Our Lady's Preparatory School, Crowthorne

How To Look After A Rodent

Rats need love
And a good home.
Gerbils need cardboard
To chew and to roam.
Hamsters like sweetcorn,
Rodents love that.
Cheerios are a favourite
For everyone's rat!

Chinchillas need grooming,
Guinea pigs sleep,
Gerbils are small,
Degus are neat.

They like sunflower seeds,
Rodent choc, cheese and more,
Their personalities so different,
So many chances to explore!

Victoria Miller (10)
Our Lady's Preparatory School, Crowthorne

Dreams

Dreams take you to exciting places
You have never been,
Like faraway galaxies, where warm foxes burrow
Or lands you have never seen.

Dreams are beams of light that change reality,
You can be a supersonic hero,
A beastly pirate or a snappy shark
Swimming in the sea.

Dreams allow you to take off and fly,
They can make you do anything if you try.
I love dreaming, it makes sleeping fun!

Eloise White (7)
Our Lady's Preparatory School, Crowthorne

Sports

S is for skating, skating is fun. You can do all sorts of moves and spins too.

P is for ping-pong. You ping and you pong in ping-pong.

O is for orienteering, running, jumping, finding, making and having fun.

R is for running, sprinting long distances.

T is for trampolining, jumping, flipping, training and fun.

S is for surfing. Testing your strength, balance and love for water.

Caitlin Ure (10)

Our Lady's Preparatory School, Crowthorne

The Rise Of The Giant Trees

Deadly still during the day,
They slowly come alive at night,
They whisper in their deep voices,
Wise eyes and sad smiles,
So many of their kind crushed by metal,
Moving mountains of brown and green,
Shaking the ground like an earthquake,
Its branches caress the morning light,
You might see them marching across rivers
and oceans.
This is the rise of the giant trees!

Jayden Berdat (7)
Our Lady's Preparatory School, Crowthorne

Mobs

Steve was yawning
In the morning
Green creepers creep
Black Endermen rise
Pale Steve flies
Awful Alex dies
Villagers trade
Creepers blow
Carrots grow
Whilst green emeralds glow
Pigs are cooked
Villagers eat some fresh meat
The Nether is a dangerous place
Because mobs rule the place
The Ender Dragon is mad
So Steve and Alex are sad.

Harry Westland (9)
Our Lady's Preparatory School, Crowthorne

Spider-Man Homecoming

In high school one day
Fighting baddies in New York at night.
His name is Peter Parker.

Spraying his webs,
Jumping off walls,
Boxing and punching,
Climbing up buildings.

He enjoys doing flips,
He is the best fighter in the world.
Some people call him Spidey,
They cheer and say,
Spidey, Spidey
Hip hip hooray.

Leo Kimani
Our Lady's Preparatory School, Crowthorne

Party All Night!

Me and my friends
Are having a disco tonight.
We're gonna have fun,
But sometimes we fight.

Then my little sister
Came in on Elliot's back.
It was really quite a shock
When Lily came in with her unicorn backpack.

After all that fun
We had to say goodbye to our friends,
But our friendship
Never ends.

Ruby Morgan (7)
Our Lady's Preparatory School, Crowthorne

My Puppy, Fred

My puppy Fred is cute and fluffy.
He's always barking.

He's scratching day and night
And loving me just right.

Fred battles his toys
And gobbles his treats.

He carries my shoes
All the way to his bed.

He likes tummy rubbing
And rolling in the dirt.
My puppy Fred.

Alyssa Alexandra McDougall (7)
Our Lady's Preparatory School, Crowthorne

The Arctic

In the Arctic
Crunching on the ground,
Is a snow leopard
Making hardly a sound.

As the leopard creeps
Around its prey,
As the polar bear sleeps
All through the day.

As the sun goes down,
As the sky goes dark,
As the polar bear rests,
As the wolves bark.

James Ferguson
Our Lady's Preparatory School, Crowthorne

The Racoon Owner

One day a boy wanted a pet,
A raccoon in his sight.
The boy said, 'Dad! Dad! I want a raccoon.'
So Dad chased the raccoon.
He finally caught it, the raccoon.
Dad put it on a leash.
The raccoon was happy.
He snuggled with his owner.
I love my pet raccoon.

Elijah Kayanja (8)
Our Lady's Preparatory School, Crowthorne

My Dog

I have a dog named Mark,
and he likes to bark.
We like to go to the park,
sometimes in the dark.
We hear the last lark,
before the stars twinkle and spark.
I love my dog Mark.

Sam Spiro (7)
Our Lady's Preparatory School, Crowthorne

Unicorns

(A diamante poem)

Unicorns
Funny, happy
Flying, bouncing, shining
Horn, wings, glitter hair, rainbow
Outstanding, singing, prancing
Friendly, pretty
Unicorns.

Chloe Norgate (7)
Our Lady's Preparatory School, Crowthorne

About A Chihuahua
(A diamante poem)

Dog
Furry, hungry
Eating, drinking, playing
Toys, bed, walks, tricks
Sleeping, running, licking
Playful, ginger
Dog.

Izzy Rae (7)
Our Lady's Preparatory School, Crowthorne

My Best Friend

She has a heart of gold.
She is as flexible as elastic.
Her voice is made of magic.
Her dream is to fly high.

Connie Wall (9)
Our Lady's Preparatory School, Crowthorne

Friendship

Friendship lasts forever.
Friendship never ends.
Friendship is together.
Friendship always mends.

Liberty-Grace Harrod (8)

Our Lady's Preparatory School, Crowthorne

My Rainbow

Sunlight and rain shine together.
Sunlight as bright as a raging fire,
Rain, as clear as a polished pane of glass,
Together they form a rainbow.

Sunlight and rain shine together.
A lovely children's fairy tale,
A pot of gold at the end,
Running for hours and hours,
Never finding anything.

Sunlight and rain shine together.
A rainbow shaped like a tall, gleaming arch,
As beautiful as an elegant swan raising its head,
Seven colours sparkling like a sunlit lake.

Sunlight and rain from a rainbow.
As red as a robin's breast,
As orange as a cunning fox,
As yellow as the gleaming sun,
As green as fresh new grass,
As blue as the never-ending sky,

As indigo as the dark depths of the night,
As violet as the juice of a blackberry,
My rainbow!

Sreevedha Bhuvaneshwaran
Park Lane Primary School, Tilehurst

If I Could Play Minecraft All Day

If I could play Minecraft all day long
I would build a giant model of my cat wearing a sarong.

In my world I would create my wildest dream
Of sheep with coats of purple, pink and green.

4 + 4 is 8 cobblestones, enough to build a furnace,
I've accidentally made a pumpkin pie flood
So don't make me feel earnest.

My favourite part of Minecraft
Is you can build whatever you want
But avoid any mobs and hackers,
TNT is real, your world could be in haunt.

So next time you play Minecraft
Please hide your precious possessions
As although the game is so much fun
Never forget these lessons:
Stay safe online!
Play sensibly and you'll be fine.

Libby Heather Jones (9)
Park Lane Primary School, Tilehurst

The Life Of Jack

It is hard and funny at school,
The weather is looking cool,
The sand is too hot,
I have buckets on my head or a pot,
I have hundreds of fidget spinners, colours,
chrome, red,
I've got a creaky bed,
I have a friend called Charlie Cook,
He loves a good book,
I have a sore back,
I've got a big backpack,
I met a good dad,
I met a boy who is very bad,
I had a very big cone,
I have very thin bones,
There's a very small table,
There's a long cable,
My mum has very big boots,
My brother does a lot of toots.

Jack Purvis (9)
Park Lane Primary School, Tilehurst

The Leopards And The Diamond

Midnight,
Lea's sleeping.
Deep in dreams.
Stomach rumbling, tumbling, grumbling,
desperate for food.
Dreaming of
diamonds!

Diamond!
Looking inside!
Injured gazelle limping.
Easy prey, leopard dinner.
Leo will be
happy!

Lea,
looking again.
Her great desire
a young wildebeest starving,
slow like sloths.
Easy-peasy

prey!

'Lea,
wake up!'
said excited Leo.
Sparkling, shiny, crystal diamond.
'See my present
for you
alone!'

Maya Dahunsi-Poulsen (9)

Park Lane Primary School, Tilehurst

Me And My Family

My name is Ruby and I'm a girl
And Bobby is my brother.
Stephen is my daddy
And Cassy is my mother.

I'm only seven and my auntie's six,
Which is kind of crazy.
I have two fish called Pinocchio and Tallulah
And once had a hamster called Daisy.

Me and Rosie are very lucky
As we'll always have each other.
Make-up and jewellery we'll always share
But she can have my brother
(Only joking, I love him really).

Ruby Allen (7)
Park Lane Primary School, Tilehurst

Amazing Art

A wesome paintings, waiting to be hung up,

M eaningful modern art in all shapes and sizes,

A bundant colours to choose,

Z ip out the imaginative ideas,

I llustrators make the book interesting,

N ow it's time to draw and paint,

G rowing impatient, waiting for it to dry.

A beautiful design in creation,

R eady to exhibit a masterpiece,

T ell wonderful stories with artwork.

Ria Ahuja (8)

Park Lane Primary School, Tilehurst

Seasons

Spring, trees blossoming
With bursts of colour
And birds tweet their melodious tune.

Summer, the sun blazing
Like a hot coal
Emerging from the horizon.

Autumn, golden leaves drop from trees,
The crisp air starts to bite
And heavy rain floods the streets.

Winter, as I open the door,
Cold air hits my face,
Fragile blades of grass crunch beneath my feet
And mountains of snow swam the streets.

Avi Srivastava (10)
Park Lane Primary School, Tilehurst

Snotty Tissues

Snotty tissues,
Where do I put them?
Under the sofa
Or feed them to the dog?

Snotty tissues in my pocket
To keep for later
To make a tissue monster.

Snotty tissues
Big, green and lumpy,
Full of goo, so lovely to lick
Mmm, needs some pepper.

Snotty tissues in my hand,
Ready to throw snot bombs at my brother.

Snotty tissues
Uh oh, I'm out of snot.

Anthony Ribbons (9)
Park Lane Primary School, Tilehurst

The Freedom Of Riding

As I gallop up the hill
Wind rushing in my eyes
Until I get a sudden chill
As my horse is harassed by the flies.

As I cantered around the field
It felt as if I was flying
As we started to speed up
I made sure my eyes were peeled
We were going so fast
My eyes watered as if I was crying.

As I approached the jump
My horse took a leap
I fell off and hurt myself
Like I was shot 1,000 times.

Amelia Sue Rain (9)
Park Lane Primary School, Tilehurst

Minecraft Life

Every morning and every night
I live a Minecraft life.
Building worlds is what I do,
My best is Towers, what about you?
Creepers creep and animals play
I wish that I could play all day!
All my friends love to play it too, together we built
a massive zoo!
Just be careful as you need to survive
You need to watch out and stay alive!
My mum says too much will hurt your eyes
But I really do love my Minecraft life!

Kyra Louise Yanni (8)
Park Lane Primary School, Tilehurst

My Cats

Milo frolics like a lamb
And gets into an awful jam.
Exploring the house and full of beans,
Sleeps a lot with twitchy dreams.

Maisy can be very vicious,
But she finds treats are quite delicious.
She is a very athletic cat
And leaves us presents on the mat.

Chippy is a grandad cat,
Legs are short and tummy fat,
Moving slowly and very loud,
He wakes the household with his miaow!

Ella Wilson (8)
Park Lane Primary School, Tilehurst

The Toad And The Rain

I walked down the road
And I saw a toad.
It looked at me with surprise!
I don't know why,
I wasn't in disguise!
We see each other every day,
When I go shopping,
Toad goes hopping,
Back to his family.
The rain does fall,
And out the toad crawls,
Enjoying his soak
Toad does a croak.
Hopping with joy,
It's time for a feast!
So let's eat
Slugs and bugs aplenty!

Demi Paris Brockbank (7)
Park Lane Primary School, Tilehurst

My Pet Unicorn

The tail and the mane of the joyful unicorn,
Were like rainbows, glistening brightly in the light.
My unicorn's swirly horn,
As bright as the burning sun,
My unicorn's beautiful wings,
As big as a greedy cow.

Unicorns fly elegantly in the sparkling sky,
My unicorn will eat precious jewels
And twinkling glitter.
My unicorn looks like a ballerina
Twirling beautifully.

Kurinji Srinivasan (8)
Park Lane Primary School, Tilehurst

Minecraft

You spawn dark in the forest or light in the town,
Plenty of zombies and creepers all around.
A lot of people frightened and scared,
They only have a little town but lots of zombies
spawn there.

There are lots of games like hide-and-seek,
You can also spawn at the Nether
And there are lots of games, whatever, whatever,
People hiding desperate to survive,
Fight them and away they fly.

Grace Annetts (9)
Park Lane Primary School, Tilehurst

Digging Around The World

Praying for enemies in the night,
Building fortresses to keep out of sight.
Looking around for danger,
Then putting them in the chamber.

Finding gold and steel,
In the desert of Creel.
Tomato covered in dragon ears
Dropping pork or tears.

Creeper! Creeper!
Never get in his way.
Build yourself a cave.
Don't become his slave.

Moksha Pallapothu (8)
Park Lane Primary School, Tilehurst

The Animal Football

Goals waiting to be hit,
Footballs waiting to be kicked,
Alone in the dark until tomorrow.

Dawn just breaks,
Animals gather on the pitch,
Everybody cheers,
I play football with someone who is cool.

The whistle is blown and there are echoes,
The game has started,
Thirsty animals run along the pitch
Determined to win.

Grace Taylor (10)
Park Lane Primary School, Tilehurst

The Deer, The Bear And The Lion

The deer is drinking beer
With Leah and Mia on the pier
With a cake with one tier.

The rare bear with fair hair
Is sitting in the chair and wants to share
The beer with the deer.

The lion who's called Ryan has an iron.
He throws the iron at the bear in his chair.
Then Ryan the lion goes to eat the deer drinking beer.

Tess Lawrence (8)
Park Lane Primary School, Tilehurst

Dreams

D reams can be lovely, sometimes bad
R ipening apples sitting on a colossal tree
E very day, lying on a bed of clouds
A fter dinner, always having ice cream
M aybe you have dreams like this
S ometimes I do.

Lily May Dimes (8)
Park Lane Primary School, Tilehurst

Darkness

Darkness, hated by all,
The dreaded darkness,
An enemy to be defeated.
Why do you scare me?
It will creep up on me.
I hate you
But I like you
Dreaded darkness.

Renae Sebogiso (10)
Park Lane Primary School, Tilehurst

My Hamster, Chubby

Chubby the hamster is adorable,
She likes to do the monkey bars,
She makes my heart beat loudly,
When I am near to my hamster
I feel spellbound.

George O'Connell (7)
Park Lane Primary School, Tilehurst

Dreams And Emotions

Minecraft dreams are twinkling stars shining in the sky.
Looking down at shimmering waters,
Come and watch me fly.
Dreams of Endermen wandering in mines.
Hurry, hurry! They are coming
And we're running out of time.

Minecraft emotions give such joy for all eternity.
Especially, flying free all alone, just me
I could cry a sea full of water
Because emotions take over me.
Anger, setting forests on fire
Whilst I fly higher and higher.

I never thought I'd give such devotion
To any of my dreams or emotions.

Erin O'Donovan (10)
St Margaret Clitherow Catholic Primary School, Pembroke

How Minecraft Works

As I enter the world
My fingers swirled,
So I started to play the game.
As I walked forward the rain
Poured but I keep on looking the same.
I looked up high into the sky
As I saw a flash of lightning,
It was frightening.
So I collected some wood,
It was used like a hood
So I should build a house.

Niamh Clyne (8)
St Margaret Clitherow Catholic Primary School, Pembroke

Creeper Run!

M ine, fight, build

I am very, very thrilled

N ever face dangers

E ndermen are the biggest changers!

C rash! Boom! The creeper explodes

R un! Run! I shout

A nd more and more they come

F wahhh, I run and run

T onight I shall not die.

Jarrell Cardoz (11)

St Margaret Clitherow Catholic Primary School, Pembroke

Surviving Minecraft

I run, I squirm like a worm.
Creepers, sleepers send me shivers.
My shelter, stairs like a helter skelter.
'Help,' I yelp.
Skeletons fire arrows.
All kinds of random things
But at last I rest,
My chest relaxes again.

Alea Doua Mchala
St Margaret Clitherow Catholic Primary School, Pembroke

Herobrine

Haiku poetry

I am Herobrine.
Peace is now an endless hope.
Fire burns in my heart.

I am a rabbit,
War is never the answer.
Just feel positive.

Valerie C Ustariz Rodriguez (10)
St Margaret Clitherow Catholic Primary School, Pembroke

The Seasons

The first season is spring
Where the birds start to sing
All the plants begin to grow
It's the first season
Now you know.

The next season is summer
Where the days begin to get warmer
After that it is autumn
And that season is truly awesome
Because it's Halloween.

It is winter that comes last
And the snow falls really fast
A blanket of snow lay below
The morning's rising sun.

Those are the seasons of the year
One, two, three and four
Now you share it with your peer
I will say no more.

Eloise Hanson (10)
Streatley CE Primary School, Streatley

Harvest

Thank you for every vegetable, every fruit
and every grain.
Thank you for all the farmers that give hours of
their lives for us,
Harvesting their crops.
Thank you for harvest.

Thank you for butternut squash and peas.
Thank you for lettuce and thyme mixed with
tomato and chives.
Thank you for all the grains we eat like barley
and wheat.
Thank you for harvest.

Thank you for strawberries and berries that attract
little birds.
Thank you for a crisp, golden apple that tastes so
nice, it melts like ice.
Thank you for red cherries and seedy blackberries.
Thank you for a cold iceberg lettuce that is nice to
eat as an ice-cold drink.
Thank you for harvest.

Thank you for a nice juicy pear that tastes so good it makes the earth quake.
Thank you for a squash that can squash bullying and squash unkindness.
Thank you for thyme because it gives time with our family and time with our friends.
Thank you for harvest.

Fergus Joseph Caulfield (10)
Streatley CE Primary School, Streatley

The Ender Game

Grabbing my axe,
Getting my dog,
Going outside,
Chopping a log.

Then all of a sudden
An Enderman came
And with his chilling voice said,
'Let's play a game!'

I was suspicious,
But needed some fun,
So I said back,
'OK, the deal is done.'

The Enderman said,
'The game is to survive.
They are coming and remember
Your dog can't retrieve.'

This was creepy,
But I had a sword

And I asked, 'Who's coming?'
'The Ender Lord!'

I saw him and his pawns
And my bones began to rattle,
But with my sword and bow
I rushed into battle.

Cai Iestyn Davies (10)
Streatley CE Primary School, Streatley

Seasons

The first season is spring,
With all the whistling birds
And all the blossoming flowers
That are as beautiful as snow.
The second season is summer,
With all the buzzing bees
And all the flowering flowers
That have lots of petals.
The third season is autumn
And all the leaves falling
And the cold puddles
With leaves turning red.
The last season is winter
With frozen lakes and seas
And snowball fights all day
And all excitement ready for Christmas Day,
This was my poem of all the seasons,
Just in case you don't know.

Joanne Roy (10)
Streatley CE Primary School, Streatley

Four Seasons Poem

Spring's the first season,
Joy and laughter comes too.
Trees and flowers come alive,
Some red, some yellow, some blue.

The next season is summer,
Bringing its lovely heat and sun.
Everybody chill out
And go and have some fun.

Falling leaves around me,
Dropping off the oak,
Autumn's overtaken
And summer's up in smoke.

Winter's coming next,
Cold breezes fill the air.
The Christmas tree looks amazing,
I'm trying not to stare.

Sacha Webb (11)
Streatley CE Primary School, Streatley

Minecraft

If you start a world
You will need some wood
And if a pig or cow turns up
Make sure to get it
So you can eat it,
Make a house
Unless you want to be slaughtered
By the creeper or the skeleton
And if you're really unlucky
You will see an Enderman,
Remember he can teleport
So watch behind you,
When it turns to day
You might need to go mining,
To find iron, gold and coal
And if you're really lucky
You might find a diamond,
The gleaming, most glamorous crystal.

Fraser Cox (10)
Streatley CE Primary School, Streatley

Mysterious Flyer

Tiptoeing through the grass,
Cutting the grass on point,
Seeing straight through the cold,
Crystal water, waiting for prey,
When the prey comes she meets its eyes,
Getting ready for the kill.
She slowly limps through the cold, slippery rocks,
Her claws gripping like a hawk on the rocks.
When she gets closer she pounces on the mouse,
Ripping it apart
And then she just plays with it
And that's because the animal
You've just read about is a cat...

Euan McInnes (11)
Streatley CE Primary School, Streatley

The Emotions

Happy
I'm so happy that the sun shines on me.
I'm so happy that everyone crowds me.

Sad
I'm so sad it starts raining.
I'm so sad and every drop of rain is just more pain.

Amazed
I'm so amazed that I could run for miles.
I'm so amazed that my eyes popped out and it hurt.

Scared
I'm so scared that I fainted.
I'm so scared that I cried for people.

Ella Von Sternberg (9)
Streatley CE Primary School, Streatley

Four Seasons

Spring's the first season,
Time to plant seeds,
Trees and flowers come alive,
Some red, yellow and blue.

Summer's second,
All so hot,
Time to cool,
Get ready for school.

Autumn's third,
Getting cool,
Time to harvest,
Eat some fruit.

Winter's last,
Get ready for Christmas,
Get a turkey,
Get presents!

Jay Radbourne (11)
Streatley CE Primary School, Streatley

Harvest

Lettuce
Let us grow crops.
Let them grow.
Let us be nice.
Let us be thankful.

Peas
Let peace dwell here.
Peace with ourselves.
Peace with one another.
Peace with the world.

Thyme
Time for ourselves.
Time for each other.
Time for our family.
Time for our friends.

Cory Forder (9)
Streatley CE Primary School, Streatley

Friendships

Friends are to help,
Friends are to care for,
Friends have fallouts,
But they get back together,
To have a friend you need to be fun,
To be a friend you need to be kind,
To lose a friend you need to be selfish,
To make a friend you need to be caring,
Friends are one of the most amazing things you
can have.

Ben Howe (10)
Streatley CE Primary School, Streatley

Minecraft

M ining with the darkness
 I n the dead of night
N ever go alone
E veryone in sight
C reepers chasing after me
R ubies are right there
A fter I've collected them
F or then I will be rich
T ill I go and sell them all and buy some empty chests!

Emily Richardson (10)
Streatley CE Primary School, Streatley

Be Who You Are

Don't be afraid to be who you are,
Don't be afraid to shine like a star,
There are people who are scared,
So their personality isn't shared.
Be who you are,
Shine like a star.
Don't let anyone change you.
You can dance,
You can sing,
You're amazing.

Elsie Waite (10)
Streatley CE Primary School, Streatley

Drawing

Pen, paper, creativity,
That's all you need to draw.
Pen, paper, creativity,
That's all you need to have fun,
Write,
Draw,
Have fun.
Pen, paper, creativity,
That's all you need to draw.
Pen, paper, creativity,
That's all you need to draw...

Jacob Steer (10)
Streatley CE Primary School, Streatley

Poetry

Poetry is wonderful,
Reading every line,
There are acrostics, free verse
And the ones that rhyme.
It's a great way to release your imagination,
It's a great way to let your mind go free,
Writing poems can be easy,
Just let loose your creativity!

Gus Dellowe (11)
Streatley CE Primary School, Streatley

My Puppy

Doggie, why are you so soggy?
Your hair is wet,
Don't go in the mud you naughty doggie.
No treats,
You naughty doggie.
Time for bed you naughty doggie.
Howling in the night, midnight strikes.
Time to get up naughty doggie.

Emily-Jayne Victoria Moore (9)
Streatley CE Primary School, Streatley

Friendship

K irsty is the best.

I love Kirsty so much.

N ice people can be my friends.

D ays are good with friends.

Annabel McLean (109)

Streatley CE Primary School, Streatley

Dinosaur Roar

Look at the compsognathus sneak away,
But lands in a waterhole with a stingray.
What's that? Oh no! It hunts in packs!
Massospondylus is sometimes bigger,
It eats cats, chomps rats and gobbles bats.
He eats diplodocus for dinner
That makes him no thinner.
He's coming this way
But he gets stuck in some clay.
It's an albertosaurus never mind,
Let's see what else I can find.
A pack of dromaeosaurus are chasing me
And I run into a tree.
I run with speed.
The dromaeosaurus get stuck in some weeds.
That's enough dinosaurs for today
But the albertosaurus gets out of the clay.
I run into a hole with a sinornithosaurus eating a mole
So I decide to run away.
I'll come back another day.

Caleb Josiah Navarro (8)
The King's House School, Windsor

Geography

G o for it, travel around the world, there's something for all to get amused by

E specially lovely beaches in Hawaii, Florida and the Maldives

O r big cities like New York, Moscow and Tokyo

G reat things can be found along the way such as pyramids in Egypt and hot springs in Iceland

R emember to invite a friend or two to go with you

A sk lots of questions before you go to know what to do and what not to do

P lease have some fun but be careful so that you come home safely

H ave a local dish or two wherever you go and learn some words in the language of that country

Y ou will have a wonderful time but will be happy to be back home, sweet home.

Leo Bello (8)

The King's House School, Windsor

Yummy, Scrummy Honey

Yummy, scrummy honey,
It sticks to my thumb!
Yummy, scrummy honey,
Yum, yum, yum!

Yummy, scrummy honey,
Runny or set.
Yummy, scrummy honey,
I'd like both, I bet!

Yummy, scrummy honey,
It is so sweet!
Yummy, scrummy honey,
It is not meat.

Yummy, scrummy honey,
It's made in the bees' hive.
Yummy, scrummy honey,
It keeps bees alive.

Abigail Simpson (10)
The King's House School, Windsor

Lions Sleep

L azy and loud, licky and proud
I mportant, a king who can sing
O n the job, hunting in the jungle
N icking animals as a meal
S tole a mole and ate it on a roll

S tay in the rumbling jungle
L oud, beating a leopard in a battle
E veryone accelerating, chasing lazy gazelle
E ntering the jungle with a roar
'P raise me!' the lion says.

Joshua Richards
The King's House School, Windsor

Cute Cats

Cats sleep in,
Cats sleep out.
A cat loves to play
Round and about.
Tickle it here,
Tickle it there,
See it jump everywhere.
Scratch and climb all the time
And she is mine!

Cute and cuddly cat
And always ready to catch a rat.
Tail and toes she licks,
Soft as a mat,
Black as coal and white as snow.

Lydija Christine Rademeyer (8)
The King's House School, Windsor

Cats, Whales And Lions

The lion roars
And then out come his sharp claws.
So look out for a lion
That is ready to roar.
So you may have a cat
Who just lies on the mat
And may not catch that pesky rat,
But the cat might some day do that.
You might know that a whale
Could crash into a sail,
Then may make it start to hail!

Harry Wood (8)
The King's House School, Windsor

Science Is Amazing!

S cience is amazing

C ool and educational

I love science because of the...

E xperiments

N uc bombs are as black as coal, they are...

C ool if they don't drop on you. I love...

E xperiments because it's exciting!

Micah Odufuwa

The King's House School, Windsor

Dogs

Dogs are cute,
Dogs are soft,
Dogs lick out of their bowls,
Dogs are yellow,
Dogs are white,
Dogs are brown,
Dogs are gold,
Dogs are helpful,
Dogs rescue people,
Dogs are life savers,
Dogs can sniff their toys,
Out of the long, wavy grass.

Hope Simpson
The King's House School, Windsor

Minecraft

M ine all day

I magine what you build

N ever stop building

E ven when you build, just have fun

C reative

R ight now you can play

A great building, you made

F un stuff

T ime to play Minecraft.

Isaac Johannes Wesley Erasmus (8)

The King's House School, Windsor

Football

F ootball is fun

O bey your coach

O verpowered kicks

T ackle the other team

B elieve you can do it

A ttack, attack, attack

L earn from others

L earn from your team captain.

Benjamin Harding (10)

The King's House School, Windsor

Friendship

F riendship is funny

R eal

I ncredible

E xcellent

N ever-ending

D eep

S pecial

H appy

I nseparable and

P rotective.

Jeshurun Ali

The King's House School, Windsor

My Dad

I have a great dad, he's called Paul,
It's so cool, because he's so very tall.
He can reach for the sky
Because he is so, so high,
That he even reached over a wall!

Reuben Andrew Harding (8)
The King's House School, Windsor

FIFA

F ootball is the best
I like to talk to my friend about it
F IFA is fun today and every day
A nd it is available all the time.

Joseph Richards (10)
The King's House School, Windsor

Lion Poem

L is for lazy king of the jungle

I is for intelligent hunter

O is for orange and golden fur

N is for noisy and powerful.

Levi Swart (7)

The King's House School, Windsor

Math

M aths I love

A division sum I love

T imes tables are great

H ave a good time doing maths.

Kian Van Der Merwe

The King's House School, Windsor

The Four Fun Seasons...

Summer,
It is the hottest season,
When the sun comes out,
It is a heater, warming up the cold air,
Wow...
Now flowers are growing! But how?

Spring,
The air is colder but not too cold,
Do you like spring? I do!
Do you want to know why?
Flowers grow everywhere!

Autumn,
Leaves everywhere, falling from trees,
Be sure to tidy up your messy garden!
Clatter, clatter, clatter...

Winter,
We're now a million miles away from summer!
When you go outside be sure to put your hat
And gloves on or you'll freeze!
The snow is as soft as a super fluffy pillow...

Arpan Kaur Atwal (10)
Willow Primary School, Fernside

Captain Duck

Pop, pop coughs the spluttering truck.
'No more petrol left,' quacks Duck.
'It's good I stopped near my friend, Goat -
He uses petrol in his boat.'
Duck rap-tap-taps at Goat's back door,
Waits a while, then taps once more.
Still no answer, so instead,
He sneaks a peek inside Goat's shed.
'Hooray!' cries Duck. 'A stroke of luck,
Petrol for my thirst truck.
I'll only take a drop or two...
Look, there's Frog! Where's he off to?
He's off to take a trip on a boat.'
'Hello!' calls Sheep.
'Hop in!' says Goat.
'There's one last thing I need to bring...
Now while I'm gone, don't pull that string!'
They check the map and pack the snack.
Then suddenly, they hear a quack.
'Ahoy there, sailors!' comes a cry.
'Is this a boating trip I spy?

If there are seas to be explored,
Make way...
Captain Duck's onboard!'

Imaan Jalil
Willow Primary School, Fernside

The Transformers

Slaying, superior robots,
Conquering terrified planets,
Guns shooting cats and dogs,
Transformers viciously annihilate cities.

Debris soaring in the sky,
Flowers weeping in terror,
Humans dashing like cheetahs, chasing their prey,
Whilst robots violently vanquish each other.

Accelerating at a million miles,
Pinning down startled snipers,
Flamboyantly flying,
Are the new tyrants of Earth.

Transformers, Transformers!
Don't get in their way,
Build yourself a fortress,
Don't become their prey!
Boom! Boom!

Hammad Khalid (11)

Willow Primary School, Fernside

Mysterious Land

I woke up in the mysterious night
Full of fear, full of fright
As I shine through the night
As I lay, the bedbugs bite.

Eyes full of tears, water wipes away
Wasted years, friendship and emotions
Pills and potions
Water blends, my fears never end.

Deep in the forest
Lays a lost creature
Wandering through the night
Full of pain, full of fright.

I was scared, I was frightened
I did not know where to go
I kept it in very close sight
Through the scary night.

Aleeza Habib (8)
Willow Primary School, Fernside

My Friend, Enderman

Enderman, Enderman
You're similar to Slenderman.
Enderman, Enderman
Why can't I look in your eyes?
Are you in disguise?
Enderman, Enderman
What is your name?
You all look the same.
Enderman, Enderman
Why do you run away?
Were you born in May?
Enderman, Enderman
Are you my friend?
Why do you live in the End?
Enderman, Enderman
I like you as much as my family.

Milena Bielawska (11)
Willow Primary School, Fernside

Dog

My parents gave me a gift,
Guess what it was?
It was a brownish, black dog.
It was a little cub.
I named it Fred.
Its eyes are black.
It has a long tail.
Its teeth are very sharp.
It's not furry.
It follows me wherever I go.
I feed him at home.
It licks my hand.
It runs here and there.
It's my best friend.

Bikramjit Singh Somal (9)
Willow Primary School, Fernside

Life In One Day!

On a sunny day
It was a funny day,
Outside I ran
To the ice cream van!
When I smelt the fresh flowers
It gave me fresh powers.
I can turn leaves
Into greenish peas!
Near to the lake
There was a snake,
At home I baked a cake
And iced the cake...
As a snake!

Bisma Zafar (8)
Willow Primary School, Fernside

Christmas Wishes

Oh Christmas Eve is near,
I hope Santa will appear,
I'm excited, it's going to be Christmas Eve.
I have hope up my sleeve,
I am filled with happiness.
I've fought away my sadness,
I hope I get the thing I desire,
So I can admire it by the fire.

Nadia Ankiewicz-Heetun (8)
Willow Primary School, Fernside

Minecraft

Redstone is red, lapis is blue,
I can always hear the cows go moo!
I love to mine, I'll mine all night
Until the creepers come into sight.
The zombies are walking,
While my doors are locking.
Off to my home,
Finally alone!

Navsirat Singh (10)
Willow Primary School, Fernside

Autumn

Leaves are falling on the ground
Twisting, twirling, round and round
Autumn is here and winter's calling
Soon, all of us will be snowballing
All of the trees will be bald
Then, as the days go by
It will start to get cold.

Skeena Zara Shah
Willow Primary School, Fernside

YOUNG WRITERS INFORMATION

We hope you have enjoyed reading this book – and that you will continue to in the coming years.

If you're a young writer who enjoys reading and creative writing, or the parent of an enthusiastic poet or story writer, do visit our website **www.youngwriters.co.uk**. Here you will find free competitions, workshops and games, as well as recommended reads, a poetry glossary and our blog.

If you would like to order further copies of this book, or any of our other titles, then please give us a call or visit **www.youngwriters.co.uk**.

Young Writers
Remus House
Coltsfoot Drive
Peterborough
PE2 9BF
(01733) 890066
info@youngwriters.co.uk